JACK THORNE

Jack's plays for the stage include *Mydidae* (Soho, 2012); *Bunny* (Underbelly, Edinburgh, 2010; Soho, 2011); *2nd May 1997* (Bush, 2009); *When You Cure Me* (Bush, 2005; Radio 3's Drama on Three, 2006); *Fanny and Faggot* (Pleasance, Edinburgh, 2004 and 2007; Finborough, 2007; English Theatre of Bruges, 2007; Trafalgar Studios, 2007); and *Stacy* (Tron, 2006; Arcola, 2007; Trafalgar Studios, 2007). His radio plays include *Left at the Angel* (Radio 4, 2007), an adaptation of *The Hunchback of Notre Dame* (2009), and an original play *People Snogging in Public Places* (Radio 3's Wire slot, 2009). He was a core writer in all three series of *Skins* (E4, Channel 4, BBC America), writing five episodes. His other TV writing includes *The Fades* (2012 BAFTA for Best Drama Series), *Shameless, Cast-Offs, This is England '86, This is England '88* (2011 Royal Television Society Award for Best Writer – Drama) and the thirty-minute drama *The Spastic King*. He wrote the short film *A Supermarket Love Song* (shown at Sundance, 2006), and the feature film *The Scouting Book for Boys*, directed by Tom Harper (Film4, Celador and Screeneast, 2009), which won him the Star of London Best Newcomer Award at the London Film Festival 2009.

Other Titles in this Series

Jack Thorne

WHEN YOU CURE ME

NICK HERN BOOKS

London

www.nickhernbooks.co.uk

A Nick Hern Book

When You Cure Me first published in Great Britain as a paperback original in 2005 by Nick Hern Books Limited, The Glasshouse, 49a Goldhawk Road, London W12 8QP

Reprinted 2009, 2011, 2012

When You Cure Me copyright © 2005 Jack Thorne

Jack Thorne has asserted his right to be identified as the author of this work

Cover image: Stem Design

Typeset by Country Setting, Kingsdown, Kent CT14 8ES
Printed and bound in Great Britain by CPI Group (UK) Ltd

A CIP catalogue record for this book is available from the British Library

ISBN   978 1 85459 901 8

When You Cure Me was first performed at The Bush Theatre, London, on 16 November 2005, with the following cast:

PETER	Samuel Barnett
RACHEL	Morven Christie
JAMES	Daniel Bayle
ALICE	Lisa McDonald
ANGELA	Gwyneth Strong

Director	Mike Bradwell
Designer	Penelope Challen
Lighting Designer	Tanya Burns
Sound Designer	Nick Manning

When You Cure Me received its first workshops as part of the National Youth Theatre's Short Nyts season in August 2004, directed by Vicky Jones. The play was subsequently commissioned by The Bush Theatre.

For Chris Thorne and Fiona Bleach

Rape and Sexual Abuse Support Centre

Our journey began in 1985 when RASASC (Rape and Sexual Abuse Support Centre) was set up in a small room above a shop in Croydon, having just two telephone lines and two staff members – all on just £100 donated by a local businessman. The sole purpose of the organisation at that time was to provide a confidential helpline that would support women and girls, fourteen years and over, who were survivors of rape and/or sexual abuse.

There was an overwhelmingly positive response to the service. We began receiving calls from women and girls all over the country, providing us with an understanding about the limited services available to survivors within the UK and Northern Ireland.

Much has changed since then. The Sapphire Units have been set up within the Metropolitan Police, ensuring that every London borough has a specially trained unit dedicated to the handling of rape and sexual abuse cases. The four Havens have been introduced in and around London – these units are 'one-stop shops' for survivors where they can go to receive medical and emotional care immediately after the rape or sexual abuse. The new Sexual Offences Bill was passed in May 2004 changing the law in such a way that the rapist now has to prove they had consent. It also expands the definition of rape to include oral and anal penetration.

RASASC has expanded its services considerably and we are very proud to operate the only confidential rape and sexual abuse helpline that is open 365 days a year. We also run a face-to-face counselling service that offers more than thirty-five sessions a week and we have recently set up an advocacy service for women and girls who are courageous enough to report the crime and go through the judicial system.

We have also increasingly become a resource for other professionals, giving talks and training to colleges, police, hospitals, social services, GPs and other support services on the subject of rape and sexual abuse. In addition we are part of an independent advisory group to the Metropolitan Police on rape as well as being a member of other local partnerships and committees. As experts in the field we are also regularly asked to advise on television scripts as well as give media interviews. All of this helps raise awareness about rape and sexual abuse and bring about improved services to survivors.

The extent to which rape and sexual abuse occurs may never be known as the statistics available are only based on reported cases. Our experience tells us that most survivors do not report these horrendous crimes. Government statistics support this as they show that only 1 in 10 survivors will actually come forward and report the rape. Even more upsetting is the fact that of the very limited number that are being reported, only 6% are actually going to court and gaining a conviction.

Equally distressing is the fact that in 2001 there were in excess of fifty support centres around the country and today there are fewer than forty. The reason: there is a desperate lack of government, local and private funding being made available to us. The government continues to believe that services of this kind should remain within the voluntary and charitable sector, limiting our access to government funding.

On a daily basis, our team of professional women are dealing with very sensitive issues that are extremely painful and difficult to hear – and at times hard to comprehend. The devastation that follows rape or sexual abuse does not stop with the survivor – it has serious implications for those that are supporting them. Relationships change, dependencies grow, psychological and physical illness often sets in and suffering for all involved increases. Few can actually comprehend the impact of this heartless and shocking crime and many choose never to think about it at all. But for those whose lives have been touched by it, there is very little that will ever compare to its destruction and pain.

It is therefore our hope that in the next twenty years, through the work that we and other organisations and centres like ours carry out, we will be able to significantly increase the support available to survivors, increase the number of people coming forward to report rape and sexual abuse, increase the number of convictions gained and motivate both the government and the public to take this seriously enough to find ways to make the UK a safer place for all.

*

As a charitable organisation, we exist on grants and donations. If you feel that you would be able to make a donation, however large or small, we would be extremely grateful. This can be done by contacting us on 020 8683 3311 or by sending a cheque to RASASC, PO Box 383, Croydon, CR9 2AW. Thank you.

www.rasasc.org.uk

The author's proceeds from sales of this book are being donated to RASASC.

Characters

PETER, *seventeen*

RACHEL, *seventeen*

JAMES, *seventeen*

ALICE, *seventeen*

ANGELA, *forty-two*

Set

A teenage girl's bedroom. The play takes place in Reading over a period of three months, from January to March.

Rachel's Injuries

Rachel has a long inflamed scar down the side of her face. Surrounding the scar is severe bruising that puffs her eye. The cut gets less inflamed as the play progresses and by Act Four there's no bruising at all, just the scar. Stiffness in the rest of her body also gradually dissipates. In particular, in Act One she has trouble with her left hand and wrist but by Act Three she's moving it as if normal. But the main damage sustained is that Rachel can't move her legs, and has very little movement in the base to the middle of her spine. She is bedbound and moving her body is very painful because the rest of her spine is forced to take a weight and pressure it's not used to, but she does have some movement and some control of her bowels.

This text went to press before the end of rehearsals so may differ slightly from the play as performed.

ACT ONE

1.1

17th January.

In the blackout.

PETER (*soft, so soft*). You awake . . .

> *The lights rise gently. She's not awake, she's just sort of stretching her mouth, so he sits back. This takes forever.*
>
> *She moves again.*

Rach . . .

> *Pause.*

Rach . . .

> *Pause.*

(*Louder.*) Rachel . . .

> *Pause. The lights are at full brightness.*

Rachel, you awake . . .

RACHEL. Wha . . .

PETER (*reaching out and touching her arm again, his hand rests on the side of the bed*). Hi.

> *Pause.*

Rachel?

RACHEL. Uh . . . Di' you?

> *She retches like she's about to throw up, but stops herself.*
>
> *Pause.*

PETER. Bad dream, or . . .

RACHEL (*she takes his hand in hers*). No.

*Pause. He tries to take his hand away, but he doesn't know
how.*

I need to pee . . .

PETER. OK.

RACHEL. I, uh . . .

PETER. Shall I call your mum or . . .

RACHEL. No. Don't call her.

PETER. OK. Are you . . .

RACHEL. Can you do it?

PETER. Really? Sure.

RACHEL. There's a pan under the bed.

PETER. OK.

*He grasps under the bed, which is pretty cluttered, for the
bedpan.*

(*Desperately casual.*) What does it look like?

RACHEL. Blue.

PETER. Yeah.

He re-emerges with it.

RACHEL. There should be a, there's a insert under there too –
just cardboard – there's a stack of them – they just slot in –
the insert should . . .

He finds the cardboard insert.

PETER. Is this . . .

RACHEL. Yeah. Pass it here, it sort of clips in.

PETER. No. I can do it . . .

*He inserts it clumsily and then he goes to the end of the bed
and lifts her legs, quite roughly. He's improvising and being
slightly rough with it, so that when he attempts to slide the
bedpan underneath, she immediately falls off.*

RACHEL (*warning*). Peter . . .

PETER. Am I . . . What?

RACHEL. You're being rough . . . a bit . . .

PETER. Oh . . .

Beat.

RACHEL. Um. My knickers . . .

PETER. Yeah.

He does so gently, and blindly, sliding them off her by the knicker straps, and being careful not to look. Then he holds the knickers, unsure of what to do with them.

RACHEL. Do you want to . . . get Mum . . .

PETER (*he puts the knickers in his pocket with confidence*). It's OK.

He hesitates and then gently lifts her legs and slides the bedpan on.

RACHEL. You have to keep hold of me, so I don't – Sorry, I don't want to slip off.

PETER. No. No. It's fine.

RACHEL. I just don't want Mum sniffing . . .

PETER. It's fine. I'm pleased.

He holds her by the hips, trying to keep this as non-sexual as possible. From the floor below we faintly hear the sound of The Archers *theme music kicking off.*

Pause. She hasn't started peeing yet, she's sweating slightly, this is very difficult.

OK?

RACHEL. Yeah.

Pause.

I'm slipping, grip tighter . . .

PETER. Like this.

RACHEL. Yeah.

PETER tightens and doesn't know which way to look, so he just looks at her, and she stares at him and they're stuck like this and it's perfect and horrible. Then, finally, she starts to pee. It's hard for her to pee, and she only gives up a pathetic amount, but it seems to make a huge clattering noise as it dribbles into the cardboard bedpan. PETER doesn't breathe until she finishes.

You need to get me the toilet tissue.

PETER. Is that . . . ? Are you balanced?

RACHEL (*she moves her own hands in order to steady herself*). Yeah.

He gently lets go, leaving her balancing on the bedpan whilst he finds the toilet paper. He finds it.

PETER. Do you . . .

RACHEL. Yeah. Give it here.

He hands her the toilet roll, she wipes herself whilst looking precariously balanced. He moves as if to help at one point, but holds back. She deposits the tissue in the bedpan.

You empty it in the toilet – and there's a bin in there – for the, uh, insert.

PETER. OK . . .

He reaches in again, helps her balance herself, and then slides her off the bedpan.

RACHEL. Don't look at it – there'll be blood . . .

PETER. OK.

He takes the bedpan out of the room, carefully averting his eyes. We're left with just her. She shifts on the bed and winces. She touches the scar on her cheek, she traces it with her fingers. She tries to shift up on the bed, but she winces again and gags, this really hurts.

(*Re-entering.*) OK . . .

RACHEL. Yeah.

> PETER *sits by her bed. They sit in silence, then she takes his hand.*

PETER. There wasn't much blood.

RACHEL. Wasn't there?

PETER. I thought you'd want to know – there wasn't . . .

> *Beat. She watches him.*

RACHEL. You need to give me my knickers back . . .

PETER (*he laughs through his nose*). Yeah. Um . . .

> *He finds the knickers in his pocket and starts putting them on her legs. He's rough again, like he was with the first attempt at the bedpan. She waits until he finishes and then moves her own hands down to straighten up his attempts.*
>
> *They sit in silence for a moment.*

I could get you some of those baby wipes. For your hands, so that when you go to the loo, you can clean them too. Because you don't want them dirty – I thought –

RACHEL. OK.

PETER. I'll get them tonight. When I leave . . . or . . .

RACHEL. Yeah. OK.

PETER. Just say when you've had enough basically . . .

> *Pause.*

RACHEL. I'm really pleased . . . you're here.

PETER. Yeah? I spoke to James last night . . .

RACHEL. OK.

PETER. He asked after you. He sounded worried.

RACHEL (*non-committal*). OK.

PETER. They've got back together, him and Alice. He sounded really pleased about it, she said some really nice stuff to him too, about it all . . .

RACHEL. OK.

They sit in silence again. PETER *takes a Ventolin asthma inhaler from his trousers and takes a squirt.*

PETER. Everyone's being really nice about it . . . you. I mean, everyone's saying nice things . . .

RACHEL (*soft*). There's no reason, for the legs – it's just me –

PETER. Yeah?

RACHEL. It'll go away –

PETER. OK.

RACHEL. They think it'll go away soon – sometimes it just does – they basically promised. Will you help me sit up . . .

PETER. Yeah. You just want another cushion behind you or . . .

RACHEL. No. Just sitting up . . .

PETER. OK.

He leans over her, and holds her by her armpits. He starts to haul her up the bed, so she's higher on the headboard. But then she screams and he stops. He doesn't speak, he just makes a noise.

Pause.

RACHEL (*getting her breath back*). It's fine.

Pause.

PETER. I didn't –

RACHEL. It's fine.

Pause. They both get their breath back.

Pull me up a bit higher, would you?

PETER. What? No! It hurts you.

RACHEL. I want to be up higher.

PETER. No, I . . .

RACHEL. Please, Peter.

PETER. Why?

RACHEL. Can you help me, please?

He gingerly fingers his arms around her armpits and attempts to pull her higher on the headboard. He starts carefully, but he has to tug her up, so he can't be gentle. She gags slightly at the effort, but manages to stop herself from screaming.

(*Again waiting a moment for breath.*) Thank you.

They sit a moment longer. PETER *is white-faced. He pulls out and takes another tug from his inhaler.*

PETER. Are you OK?

RACHEL. I feel older, do you know that?

PETER. Yeah? I don't particularly. Is that –

Beat.

RACHEL. Will you get in with me?

PETER. Yeah?

RACHEL. Will you . . .

PETER. It won't hurt?

RACHEL. No.

Beat.

PETER. That wasn't what that was about, was it? Getting up higher.

RACHEL. No.

PETER. You weren't making it so I could get in. Moving up, so . . .

RACHEL. Will you get in?

PETER. Yeah.

He squeezes himself onto the bed, so that his hips are just on the side of the bed. She pulls him in closer, and partly curls what parts of the body she can around him.

Can you, uh –

RACHEL. This is nice.

PETER. Yeah.

RACHEL. I can feel your heartbeat, it's going quick actually . . .

PETER. Is it?

RACHEL. Yeah. (*She takes his hand and puts it on his heart.*)

PETER. Yeah.

RACHEL. You're nervous, that's all –

> *Beat.*

> (*Soft.*) Do you mind the scar?

PETER. No.

RACHEL. It'll fade. I mean, I'll look the same . . .

PETER. You're really pretty. You still are.

> *Beat.*

RACHEL. This is nice. I like it like this.

> *She feels her hand around and sort of pats him.*

PETER (*giggle*). Oh. Um. Mr Norris asked if you wanted work set, by the way. (*She giggles.*) And Mr Edwards, though he was weird about it, he said I had to talk to him, well, if I wanted to, and that I had to call him Geoff . . .

RACHEL (*giggle*). Geoff!

PETER (*giggle*). Yeah.

> *Pause. She tries to snuggle up.*

RACHEL. I'm really happy just like this . . .

PETER. Yeah.

RACHEL. Geoff!

PETER (*giggle*). Yeah.

RACHEL. What did you do?

PETER. I don't know. Ran away.

> *She smiles. Pause, a long luxury pause. They breathe into each other.*

RACHEL. I wish we could just stay like this . . .

PETER. Yeah.

Pause.

RACHEL (*she suddenly whitens*). Peter. Is that . . . Peter. Have you got an erection?

PETER. No.

He shifts his groin backwards.

RACHEL. Yes. Ow.

PETER. No.

RACHEL. Peter – you can't – ow –

PETER. I can't – I'm sorry –

He moves his arms back, he tries to find space, he can't. She growls like a cat, pure frustration. He's almost in tears.

Sorry – I can't . . .

RACHEL. I can FEEL it – uh – uh –

He's trying to pull everything away from her.

PETER. Don't, don't, I'm sorry. I'm sorry.

Beat.

I'm sorry.

Beat. He's as far back as he can be, yet he still flurries some more, trying to find more space.

I'm so sorry. Rachel . . . Rachel . . .

RACHEL (*half-spoken*). OK.

Beat. She's struggling to control her tears. He concentrates on holding his stomach in.

PETER. Sorry –

RACHEL. No.

PETER. Sorry, shall I get off –

Beat.

RACHEL. Hold me.

PETER. Sorry. I'm so sorry.

Pause. She moves towards him. He tries to evade as much of her as possible, but she's more aggressive than he is.

Pause.

RACHEL. No. Get off.

PETER. Sorry. I'm really . . .

He half-falls off the bed in relief.

It's not. It doesn't mean I expect . . . it's not like a signal or . . .

Beat. She can't speak. He tries to stand in a way that minimises the erection. He takes another squirt from his inhaler, he's in a panic.

I'm really really sorry, I just don't know what to do . . . That's all. Sorry.

Beat.

RACHEL (*swallow*). OK.

PETER. I feel sick. I'm really sorry.

Pause. PETER can't decide whether to leave or not. He's determined not to look at the door until he does.

(*Soft, his mouth doesn't work properly.*) I'm not sure what I'm supposed to do . . .

Pause. He straightens his back, the erection has finally subsided.

Rachel . . .

Pause.

Rach . . .

RACHEL (*she looks up finally, meets his face*). Yeah?

PETER. Sorry? Sorry.

Blackout.

1.2

21st January.

JAMES *and* ALICE *are beautiful people.* RACHEL *is enjoying them, despite herself.* PETER *is a little cluttered. All except* RACHEL *wear school uniform.*

JAMES. . . . He was having a go and he put his hand down her trousers and he couldn't find what he was looking for so he kept looking and then he put his finger in, but it wasn't the right hole –

RACHEL. What?

JAMES. Went for the pink and potted the brown, Mary Gill, though this isn't from either of them. Anyway, so she slapped him.

ALICE. Did she?

JAMES. Didn't I tell you this? Yeah. Apparently she slapped him.

RACHEL. Mary?

JAMES. Yeah.

ALICE. She's fancied him for ages.

JAMES *(he opens his bag and brings out cheap vodka).* Well, he's not going near her now – probably not until he smelt his finger that he realised. *(He takes a swig of the vodka.)* Actually, he smelt his finger and he's either realised, or he thinks she's seriously unwell, can you drink?

RACHEL. Yeah.

PETER. What?

JAMES *(mimicking PETER as he hands her the bottle).* 'What?' Have you got any music?

PETER. James –

RACHEL *(to PETER).* What? *(To JAMES.)* Nothing good.

JAMES *(laughs).* I'll find something.

RACHEL. OK.

PETER *sits down on the side of the bed. He turns on the bedside light beside* RACHEL, *then looks around at the rest of the room and turns the light off again.* ALICE *smiles at him.* RACHEL *looks at* ALICE. ALICE *doesn't know what to say.*

ALICE (*gesturing the vodka bottle*). Can I borrow that?

RACHEL. Yeah.

ALICE *takes a swig.* PETER *stands up and tucks an errant bit of sheet in, with a complicated smile.*

ALICE. Suzy and Mike have finally got together –

RACHEL. Have they?

ALICE. Yeah.

RACHEL. I don't really know Suzy that well . . .

ALICE. Oh, she's great, I should introduce you –

RACHEL. Yeah, I've met her.

ALICE. No. I mean, you should, you should definitely come out with us sometime –

RACHEL. OK.

PETER. Girls' night out? You should definitely do that.

ALICE (*swinging a grateful grin in* PETER*'s direction*). So you'll come?

RACHEL. OK.

ALICE. Brilliant.

JAMES. This is a shit music collection, you know –

PETER. James –

RACHEL. Yeah, I know.

JAMES. Pete, take an interest, mate, sort your girlfriend's music collection out.

RACHEL. Yeah.

JAMES. No, I'm not being serious. Your mum's really lovely, by the way, she tried to invite us to dinner –

RACHEL. Did she?

JAMES. Yeah.

Beat. JAMES tries to touch ALICE surreptitiously. RACHEL notices. ALICE notices RACHEL notice and steps away from her boyfriend's grasp.

Pause. RACHEL smiles. She looks at ALICE directly. JAMES notices and takes a step away from ALICE, and then, because he doesn't want it to look obvious, he takes another step, and then he walks to the other side of the room.

This is nice, this room –

ALICE. This is really nice actually –

JAMES (*turning to his girlfriend, all hips*). Which is different from nice how?

ALICE. What?

PETER. By being 'really' nice I think, mate . . .

JAMES (*small exclusive chuckle*). OK.

ALICE. We think Mr Taylor might have been sacked.

RACHEL. Yeah?

JAMES. Well. Yeah. Alice thinks he might have touched up Rebecca –

ALICE. She's been telling him about her period.

JAMES. Apparently he's 'really good to talk to'. Which means he's a pervert. I mean, she's got nothing even to talk about neither – though it could be her period, I suppose, if there's some discharge in it – he's a pervert whatever, I think. Anyway, he's off at the moment, someone's taking his lessons –

PETER (*turning to RACHEL*). Are you OK?

RACHEL (*with a funny face*). Yes.

PETER. It's good, isn't it? Having everyone here –

RACHEL. Is it?

JAMES. Leave her alone, mate . . .

PETER. What?

JAMES (*to* RACHEL). More vodka?

Beat. He takes the vodka from ALICE, *who lets him, and gives it to* RACHEL, *who lets him. She wipes the lid and has a swig.* PETER *then tries to take it from her, and she reluctantly lets him. He puts it on the chest of drawers, away from everyone.*

Oh, and Colin Jackson is coming to school, that's the other thing, to do prize-giving – Nightingale's really excited – it's really funny actually – he's not Colin Jackson, he's 'World-Record-Holder Colin Jackson'. He's given an assembly about you too –

RACHEL. Has he?

JAMES. Yeah.

ALICE. We had a policeman come in and tell us about safety and everything –

RACHEL. Who?

PETER tugs on his asthma inhaler. He looks around to see if anyone's watching him. JAMES *moves over towards the vodka.*

ALICE. The policeman?

RACHEL. Yeah.

ALICE. I don't know.

RACHEL. OK.

PETER. I wasn't there, it was just for the girls . . .

Beat. ALICE *walks over to where* JAMES *is, just because she wants to stand close to him.* JAMES *picks up a hairclip from the top of* RACHEL*'s chest of drawers, studiously avoiding the vodka. He puts the hairclip down again. He fiddles with one of the drawer knobs, but he doesn't open anything.*

JAMES. Everyone's been talking about you . . .

RACHEL. Saying what?

ALICE. Just loads of nice stuff.

JAMES. Pretending you're their best friend. It was getting boring . . . I mean, it's stopped now basically . . .

RACHEL. Yeah?

JAMES. Everyone's been really dumb about it.

RACHEL. Yeah.

Pause. ALICE *takes* JAMES*'s hand.* PETER *moves closer to* RACHEL.

JAMES. Has the police said anything?

Beat.

RACHEL. No. Not much. I'm just – we did . . . a photofit.

JAMES. How come they aren't showing that around the school then?

RACHEL. I don't know.

JAMES. Probably just want to catch him, that's what's wrong with the whole thing actually. They should be showing us and saying, 'Fuck catching him, let's just prevent this happening to more girls.' Shouldn't they?

RACHEL. I don't know.

JAMES. Not my problem, I suppose. How come you don't have a TV up here?

RACHEL. I didn't want one.

JAMES. So what do you do? When Peter's not here –

RACHEL. Oh. I can't remember.

Beat.

ALICE. OK.

Beat. PETER *wakes up and moves half a step closer to* RACHEL, *both* JAMES *and* ALICE *watch him. Then*

RACHEL*'s mobile phone goes off. She picks it up and rejects the call.*

PETER. Who was it?

RACHEL. I didn't know the number . . .

PETER. It could have been the police . . .

RACHEL. No.

JAMES. Listen to him! All responsible now, are you, Petey? Peter told you about county trials . . . Baylis thinks he's a shoo-in . . .

PETER. No. I'm not –

JAMES. He couldn't get picked for the school team before this year. I think he did a soccer-skills thing during the summer and never told anyone –

RACHEL (*to* PETER). You didn't tell me – That's good, isn't it?

JAMES. Yeah. It is.

PETER. It doesn't mean anything.

JAMES. You watch him. He'll get the lead in the musical next –

ALICE (*giggle*). We watched them do the auditions, you could just sit there if you were auditioning too, so we just sat there . . .

PETER. You auditioned?

JAMES. No, mate, you go for it. It was funny watching though – (*Sings.*) 'Maybe this time . . . '

ALICE. It was pathetic.

JAMES *checks his watch,* RACHEL *notices him. He notices* RACHEL *noticing him and blushes.*

RACHEL. You better go. I'm pretty tired.

PETER. Yeah. She's pretty tired.

Beat. JAMES *shrinks slightly.* ALICE *dwindles too.* RACHEL, *annoyed with* PETER, *tries to help them.*

RACHEL. Going somewhere nice?

ALICE. No. Everyone's just meeting at The Dog and Goat.

RACHEL. Are you going, Peter?

PETER. No.

JAMES. Aren't you? OK.

Pause.

ALICE. Are you two closer? Would you say? Now this has all happened? I mean, me and Jay got closer just because when he got ill, I went round there a lot. But that wasn't a proper illness . . .

RACHEL. Yeah?

Pause.

JAMES. We got closer because she let me shag her but she won't say that –

ALICE (*giggles*). Shut up.

Pause. JAMES moves closer to ALICE, ALICE sways towards him.

JAMES. There's nothing we can do, by the way? Like, you want lifting or anything . . .

Pause. RACHEL looks at PETER accusingly.

RACHEL. Where?

JAMES (*looking at PETER too. Laughs*). I don't know.

Pause.

PETER. I think everything's fine, isn't it?

RACHEL. Is it?

JAMES (*laying it on thick*). Is it?

PETER. Yeah. I mean, I don't know.

RACHEL. Yeah. It's fine.

PETER. OK.

Blackout.

1.3

24th January.

PETER *is sitting watching* RACHEL *sleep. He doesn't move a muscle. He just sits in his seat and watches her. It's dark, we can barely see anything.*

ANGELA *enters ever so quietly.*

ANGELA. She asleep?

PETER. Yeah.

> ANGELA *moves to the bed and sits gently beside her daughter. She traces her daughter's outline with her hand. But she never touches her.* PETER *just watches, unsure what to do.*

ANGELA. How is she?

PETER. Yeah. OK.

ANGELA. You're speaking quite loudly, Peter –

> *Beat.* PETER *lowers his head slightly.*

> (*Trying to correct herself.*) Arsched says this is all perfectly normal –

PETER. Yeah?

> *Pause. She silently pulls up a chair and sits beside him.*

ANGELA. You know better than any of us really . . .

PETER. Yeah?

ANGELA. Well, that's a good thing, isn't it? Will you call me Angela, Peter?

PETER. What? OK.

ANGELA. They all call, and she says she won't have them. All her other friends . . .

PETER. Yeah?

ANGELA (*she gets up from her chair*). Have the police spoken to you?

PETER. No.

ANGELA. I keep phoning them up. I imagine it's really
very annoying for them. Rachel doesn't seem that . . .
worried. Still, I suppose that's perfectly natural. She doesn't
want me involved. Social services sit with her whenever
they come. Arsched says it'll all be OK with that. The
police are very kind about it too. I just want him caught,
you know.

Pause. ANGELA *circles* RACHEL *slightly, she's now
closer to* PETER.

Now. (*Small presumptive sniff.*) Do you . . . kiss . . . still?

PETER. What?

ANGELA. I, uh, it's not my business, but I still want her to
still be normal . . . with you . . . I know she's making you
do . . . you're having to nurse her. You're doing brilliantly.

PETER. Yeah?

ANGELA. Arsched tells me to respect what she wants. But I
know I should be up here.

PETER. I'm not, really. I mean, we're pretty normal . . .

ANGELA (*quiet*). Will you try and get her to talk to me?

PETER. Yeah? I think, I mean, I don't want to upset her . . .

ANGELA. OK.

PETER. Sorry. I mean, yeah . . .

Beat.

ANGELA. It is quite . . . strange . . . isn't it – why she wants
you here?

PETER. Yeah?

ANGELA. They tell me she can't move her legs because she's
afraid of her . . . vagina. Of the whole . . . sex, of her sex.
And if that's true then why does she want her boyfriend
here? I think you're doing brilliantly though . . . you really
are . . .

ANGELA gets up and walks to the door. PETER takes a tug on his inhaler. The lights start to slowly fade.

(*She speaks so quietly it's difficult to make out what she says.*) You're right, I don't want her getting upset, if she wakes up . . . finds me . . .

PETER. No. I didn't mean that.

ANGELA. No . . . you're right.

Pause. She's finding it really difficult to leave. PETER looks round at her.

I sometimes think we should force her – just tell her they can work – because they can – medically – but then they tell me that this is medical too – her thinking her leg's dead is somehow . . . medical . . .

PETER. She's going to get better.

ANGELA. I know . . .

PETER. No. I mean, you've, uh . . . I'm going to try really hard . . .

ANGELA. OK. Well. Come down when you're ready.

PETER. I'm going to make sure she gets better. I know what I'm doing. Really . . .

ANGELA. OK. I'll cook you something if you like.

The lights are in blackout. ANGELA exits.

PETER. OK.

ACT TWO

2.1

30th January.

The lights ping on, full beam. The scene change is instant (there is nothing to change, though perhaps RACHEL*'s duvet has been pulled up over her feet – just slightly).* PETER *is standing where the previous scene left him.*

RACHEL (*soft, she can't get enough liquid in her mouth, every time she opens her mouth we can hear it – a soft shtick on every word*). He had a knife, he said, I didn't see that 'til – he just told me, I didn't see it 'til later. And he just stood in the . . . path, and he said about the knife, and then 'You've got to follow me.' Polite and everything, very . . . honest. He said I had to follow him. That he wasn't . . . He wasn't going to be behind me, he was going to be in front of me and that I had to follow him. So I did, he was maybe three or four steps in front and I was just – following – and we came to this small – there was some swings and some – this big – and he took me to basically a shed, I followed him, to, I don't know, a shed, basically, I mean, probably the allotments, but not, definite, and he turned a light on, it was this – bulb – and then, like, undress . . .

Pause. She paddles backwards with her shoulder, she turns as if to look at him. He turns towards her too. But they don't quite make it. She paddles with her shoulder again.

(*Her voice is full of snot.*) And then he, uh – (*She clears her throat, it doesn't work, she clears her throat again.*) I wish I could – I can't even see the inside of . . . it. I mean, it could be a shed or a . . . it could have be . . . They can't even find it.

Pause. Both of them keep very still now, as if being judged.

PETER (*soft, flicking himself out of the softness*). You don't have to – tell me . . .

RACHEL. I had to stand in there – I had to be slow, taking off the clothes, I can't remember how he said it, but he told me which bits he wanted off first . . . He spoke really detailed . . .

Beat.

He said – uh, he wanted my T-shirt off – saying how he wished it was a shirt, he liked buttons . . . How can I remember this and not the – shed? And then he wouldn't let me take off my underwear for ages because he said he liked that. He kept telling me what he liked. And I threw up sometimes and he made me clean it up with my T-shirt. He tried to do it through my knickers because – and then he asked if it was my first time, saying he was pleased it was him because he could – appreciate it. And he put his fingers all over me, I remember these . . . they were so scratchy, like, old skin and, he never used his nails.

Pause. She looks up at him, frightened. He takes a tug on his inhaler, she watches him.

Do you want to know the worst bit? Do – you – that sounds such a – but . . . (*Giggle.*) The worst bit was – was when the doctors examined me afterwards, because then I felt it . . . all. They put me in this room, they call it a suite but it's a room – the police – and then the doctors come and . . . They had to – take samples from me – my – me – vagina, my . . . bum, my mouth, my – they had to take cuttings of my pube . . . And the doctor had this latex, his breath smelt of latex too – or rubber or whatever it is – like an uncle with his face up close . . . It felt like the dentist. It was then . . . after . . . that I couldn't get off the table, they couldn't get me off. It was then my legs didn't work. And he just smiled and then frowned. And there was this woman, police officer, and she was just sitting there watching it as if he was normal. And that was the . . . Is that terrible? That that's the . . . That I think that?

Beat.

Peter?

PETER. I don't . . . Have you got – is there anything I can ask?

RACHEL. What?

PETER. For – the – is there anything you'd like me to ask? Anything you want me to know but want me to ask the questions for?

RACHEL. What?

PETER. It just feels like you want me to ask something . . .

RACHEL. No –

PETER. It sounded as if you weren't saying something.

RACHEL. I said everything.

She reaches out a hand to him, but he doesn't meet it. So she turns it into a hand reaching for a cup, she drains it. He walks to the foot of her bed, and pulls the duvet over her toes, before coming back up the bed to stand beside her.

PETER. Shall I get some more water?

Pause. She looks at him carefully.

I'm really pleased you told me. I think it's important. Yeah.

RACHEL. He, uh, he helped me clean up afterwards. He found some – cloth – my T-shirt or . . . I don't know. I couldn't even feel it but he – I couldn't stop bleeding and he . . . And then I said that I wouldn't tell anyone, I said I didn't want him to tell anyone, that was so he could believe the lie. Because it was shameful, I said. Because I thought he could kill me otherwise. An' then he took the knife and he said 'Just as a reminder' . . .

PETER. My / mum . . .

RACHEL. I told him he had to help me by keeping it a secret, I had blood on my face, and he said he would and he sort of – patted – the side of my – face . . . and then he started punching where he'd cut, to make sure it scarred, he said . . . just punching . . . but the doctors say it'll be OK . . . and he didn't break anything . . .

Beat.

PETER. Do you want to . . . talk . . . I mean, it must have been
  pretty bad, so we could – we could talk about this stuff. Just
  talk it out.

RACHEL. OK. Aren't we doing that?

PETER. No. Listen, I've been thinking about – I was thinking I
  should like sit in on your sessions with Arsched – I want to
  be part of making you better . . .

RACHEL. Why?

PETER. I just mean, well, I'm here, aren't I?

RACHEL. I know . . .

PETER. No, I just think I should come along, it's only fair . . .

RACHEL. Fair?

PETER. No, I mean, really help you. With the police too, I
  mean, you've told me everything so I could come to that.
  I know now, I won't judge, I can be a better support than all
  of them. I mean, it must be hard you saying it all the time
  and you know that I won't – that I know it now so I could
  be there – to support you . . .

RACHEL (*quiet*). But I don't want that.

PETER. It's just that when Mum got sick – I used to go to the
  therapist's and everything with her all the time. Sometimes
  they'd talk alone but mostly I'd go in with her – and I was
  only eight or something then . . . Just sitting in, you know.

*Pause. She picks up a hairbrush from beside her bed and
begins to brush her hair. He watches her carefully.*

That's why I think I could be helping more . . . with you . . .

Pause.

RACHEL. Arsched told me, I'd decided you were safe . . .
  I don't know why I did that . . . sexually, I mean, safe. He
  reckons I can't move my legs because I said in my head
  I wanted to be safe from sex. He said I must have decided
  you were safe too . . . sexually . . .

Beat.

PETER. I talked to Alice actually, and she – before, I haven't told her the stuff that – I mean, she's great to talk to – I mean, I just think talking it out helps, I think I could really help . . .

RACHEL. What did you say to her?

PETER. I don't know. I didn't know most of the stuff, did I? Just, I don't know, how I was feeling . . . I don't know. I mean –

RACHEL. I'm not jealous, Peter. I don't think you're her type –

PETER. No . . . Look, she really likes you – she said how much she liked you, when she, uh –

RACHEL. Peter, that's just something someone like her would say –

Pause. PETER *shifts his chair forward, it makes a funny noise, he looks down to where the noise is coming from, he can't work it out.*

PETER. Well, that's not important – I want to be involved, that's all I'm saying, I'd be really good at helping you, I could really support you. (*Spilling.*) Rachel, what happened – with the – I know we didn't talk about it – but I don't want you to worry about that. I can control that.

RACHEL. What?

PETER. I just was lying really close to you – and you're really pretty – it won't happen again.

RACHEL. It doesn't matter.

PETER. It won't happen again, I know what I'm doing, just – let me be part of it . . .

Knock on the door.

ANGELA. Kids?

RACHEL. Mum . . .

ANGELA (*opening the door*). Hi. Is this OK?

RACHEL. No.

ANGELA. I've got your washing –

RACHEL says nothing. ANGELA carries the basket of washing over to RACHEL's chest of drawers.

So what have you two been up to –

RACHEL. Peter can put that away . . .

ANGELA. I'm sure Peter doesn't want to put your underwear away for you . . .

PETER. I don't mind.

Beat.

ANGELA. Hello Peter.

PETER. Hi. Do you want me to –

RACHEL. See? He can do it.

Pause. ANGELA puts the basket down on top of the chest of drawers.

ANGELA. I can't just sit downstairs –

RACHEL (*exploding*). SO GET YOUR OWN LIFE!

ANGELA. Rachel –

RACHEL. WHAT?

Pause. ANGELA thinks a moment, and then leaves.

ANGELA. I'll see you downstairs, Peter . . .

RACHEL. Will you?

Pause. RACHEL listens for the footsteps going down the stairs.

She's so . . . big, all the time . . . and then being so 'I'll see you downstairs, Peter' making herself sound big . . . You better go.

PETER. What?

RACHEL. I want to be on my own for a little bit.

PETER. Why?

Pause. He walks over to her chest of drawers and starts looking at unpacking the laundry. He picks up a pair of knickers.

RACHEL. I mean it, Peter . . .

He puts down the pair of knickers

PETER. But I want to stay up here . . .

RACHEL. Well, I can't leave, can I?

PETER. What?

RACHEL (*mimicking*). 'What?'

Pause.

PETER. I just think you're being unfair, to me, to Angela . . .

RACHEL. Angela?

PETER. What? Listen. As long as I haven't done anything wrong . . .

RACHEL. 'Angela'?

Pause. She touches her scar.

PETER. Look, today was a good day, OK? Let's not ruin things by fighting about things that aren't really important – I think – I'm going to stay for a bit . . .

Pause. She pushes her arm under her pillow.

Are you OK then?

Blackout.

2.2

2nd February.

ALICE *is sitting in the room. She's a bit fidgety and entirely different without* JAMES *to chaperone her speaking.*

ALICE. But then we talked all about that, and he didn't even like that, he thought I liked it, which is why he invited me. Or he said that, I'm not sure if I believe him really –

RACHEL. OK.

ALICE. He could be lying because he doesn't want us to split up, so he wants to pretend there isn't a problem. Anyway, we're going to try spending more time together –

Pause.

Your face is healing well, isn't it?

RACHEL (*she wants to touch her scar, but she doesn't*). Yeah.

ALICE. Do you want me to bring some make-up? Cover-stick, that sort of thing . . .

RACHEL. No.

ALICE. My mum said she wanted to buy a present for you, when she heard about it, so I could get her to pay.

RACHEL. No. Is Peter OK? At school?

ALICE. Yeah, he's great. Everyone's treating him a bit like – like he's special, because of what happened and because he's being, you know, so supportive for you. I mean, he is special, isn't he? He was brilliant to talk to about the whole James thing – I mean, because he understands what James is really like, you know –

RACHEL. Yeah.

ALICE. I mean, they're not getting on great at the moment, but they've been friends for so long, I mean, far longer than either of us have been around – with them –

RACHEL. Yeah.

ALICE. So they'll be friends again, though my mum said, when I talked to her about it, that she doesn't really know that many friends from school, which I found really weird. It'll be quite funny really if we stop being friends and then we meet up again later, at a reunion or whatever. Though she said she hadn't had any school reunions either. We've got to have a school reunion, I think. In ten years or whatever, I mean . . . I mean, my mum isn't even bothering with the website thing or anything like that, but I'd LOVE to know what everyone's doing in ten years, it'd be so interesting . . .

RACHEL. Yeah.

ALICE. You think so?

RACHEL. Is Peter the same though – as he was?

ALICE. Yeah, I mean, everyone's really giving him respect. I mean, I'm sure he'd like it better if you were around, but you still get to see each other loads, don't you?

RACHEL. Not the way we were . . . no.

ALICE. Does it seem really long ago now?

RACHEL. What?

ALICE. Well, when it all started –

RACHEL. When I was . . . attacked?

ALICE. Yeah.

RACHEL. No.

ALICE. It seems really long ago to me –

RACHEL. Does it?

ALICE. I suppose you've been here mostly. But Peter said you might come down for the trials –

RACHEL. Did he?

ALICE. Yeah. James is going now, having a go now, so I'm going to go too. Did you hear about all that?

RACHEL. What?

ALICE. Mr Baylis was a wanker and said that he shouldn't do
the trials, but James thought about it and said he was at
least as good as the other players going, and it's open trials
anyway, it's not even proper. Did Peter tell you about that?

RACHEL. No.

ALICE. I think he's pleased, that James is going –

RACHEL. Probably.

ALICE. I thought about not going – because of what we
decided – about me not having to be with him all the time –
doing girls' nights and stuff like that – which you have to
come to, by the way – and then I thought that I'd actually
quite like to see the trials – because when stuff like that's
important, you know – I mean, you're going even and
you're basically here most of the time –

RACHEL. If I'm better –

ALICE. Really? Oh, Peter said it like it was definite. He said
you were getting so much better so quickly. He said he
could almost see it – how much better you were getting. Or
that may be me thinking that, and he didn't say that at all.
I don't think Peter says things like that – but he definitely
said you were getting tons better. Well. It doesn't matter. It's
funny, isn't it? How we never used to be friends – I mean,
even with James and Peter being –

RACHEL. We don't need to be friends.

Pause.

ALICE. Are you seeing a psychiatrist?

RACHEL. Psychologist.

ALICE. I had a feeling about that. What's that like? That's not
rude, is it – it's just I knew a girl – who had to use one. A
cousin of my mum's. She fell in love with hers.

RACHEL. Arsched's fifty.

ALICE (*laugh*). Oh. OK. Oh, I'm doing the musical *Cabaret*. I
got a part.

RACHEL. Did you?

ALICE. Yeah, weird, isn't it?

RACHEL. No.

ALICE. I just went afterwards . . . don't tell James . . . It's not a big part . . . well, it's quite big.

RACHEL. OK.

ALICE. He's waiting downstairs, by the way. Do you want him to come up?

RACHEL. Who?

ALICE. James. Just don't tell him about the musical.

RACHEL. He's downstairs . . .

ALICE. Don't worry, he won't come up . . .

RACHEL. What?

ALICE. Or I could go? You know, if you're bored or anything, I don't mind – It's weird, isn't it? Because basically I only normally see you with James and Peter – He's really sweet, you know, James –

RACHEL. Yeah.

ALICE. I know you don't like him but I think the four of us could be really good friends, it's just you've got to catch him when he's being funny. I mean, he likes you, he thinks you're really nice –

RACHEL. When did you lose . . . your virginity?

ALICE. Oh.

RACHEL. It's just – I know I was later than everyone else . . .

ALICE. Not that later – I mean . . . Everyone lies about that stuff, don't they? I know Michelle Milsom didn't lose hers at fourteen and she says she did.

RACHEL. I hadn't – before the . . .

ALICE. Oh.

RACHEL. Yeah. I suppose, at least it's over with . . .

ALICE. It feels odd, doesn't it? I mean, obviously it was
different and everything . . .

RACHEL. Yeah, it is.

Beat.

ALICE. Can I do anything?

RACHEL. What?

ALICE. No. It doesn't matter.

Pause. JAMES *appears in the doorway, neither of them
notice him.*

JAMES. Your mum wanted to ask if we wanted dinner, she's
going to cook . . . But I said we probably should go . . . Hi.
Rachel. I mean – do you want to go straight away or, you
know, I could chat a bit . . .

RACHEL. Hi.

JAMES. Yeah. Peter said you just wanted to chat to Alice
really . . .

ALICE. No. He just said you wanted to talk to a girl . . .

RACHEL. Did he?

JAMES. Yeah. I got that actually – I mean, Peter probably talks
about the same stuff I do. I mean, you and Alice have
probably got more in common.

ALICE. Yeah.

Pause. RACHEL *squeezes her head around to look at*
ALICE.

RACHEL. He asked you to come?

ALICE. I wanted to – and then he said you could do with
talking to a girl, and I thought that was – brilliant. Though
James wasn't supposed to come up . . .

JAMES. I'm allowed to come up!

RACHEL. He shouldn't have asked you.

ALICE. I was really pleased though.

Pause.

JAMES. He's not about then?

RACHEL. No. He's doing some football thing . . .

JAMES. Is he?

RACHEL. Yeah. I mean . . . That's what he said . . .

JAMES (*laugh*). Well, it's not another girl . . .

RACHEL. Yeah, I know . . .

JAMES. He's probably getting you a present or something. (*Laugh.*) Or doing the football thing, of course . . .

RACHEL. Yeah.

JAMES. It's probably a football thing. I just hadn't heard about it.

RACHEL. Yeah.

JAMES. Did he . . . get picked?

RACHEL. For what?

JAMES. OK. Doesn't matter . . .

RACHEL. OK.

Pause.

JAMES. He's doing alright, though, with you? Being supportive and everything?

RACHEL. Yeah.

JAMES. Good. I was a bit worried he was going to be a wanker.

Blackout.

2.3

7th February.

RACHEL *is asleep.* ANGELA *is sitting beside her.* PETER *enters with two cups of tea, one of which he puts beside* ANGELA*'s chair, on the floor. He has to bend down far too far to get it there, making a hugely concerted effort not to spill anything, whilst still holding the other cup, it looks quite comical.*

ANGELA. Thanks, love.

Pause. PETER *sits down.*

PETER. Is she . . . uh?

ANGELA (*she can't take her eyes off her daughter*). Her dad always used to let her fall asleep on the sofa. Watching the TV, sometimes, not all the time. He only did it because he liked carrying her upstairs to bed.

PETER. Yeah?

ANGELA. They looked very . . . gentle together . . .

PETER. I wish I'd met him . . .

ANGELA. Don't – there's something about remembering that always makes you remember it better. I remember – after Ian . . . died – I wrote a note to myself saying don't think he was brilliant –

PETER. Yeah?

ANGELA. You've got to remember that, otherwise you didn't love them. It must be the same with you and Rachel, you might only remember how great it was before . . . well. Whatever it was before . . . But you certainly seemed – I thought you were a good boyfriend.

PETER. OK.

ANGELA. I phoned your mum, to say how great you're being, to check you're OK at home, because this must be difficult for you. Well, just so she knows . . .

PETER. Yeah, she said. You didn't need to do that . . .

ANGELA. She seemed pleased.

PETER. She was OK?

ANGELA. Yeah.

PETER. OK, I thought she'd been rude.

ANGELA. No, very pleasant.

PETER. She sounded like she'd been rude, when she told me about it.

ANGELA. No. She's had some difficult times . . . from what Rachel told me. Not much, obviously.

PETER. Not that difficult.

Pause.

I phoned the police . . .

ANGELA. Did you?

PETER. To ask if I could help. They said no.

ANGELA. OK.

PETER. Yeah, I mean, they said it was going fine.

ANGELA. It's not.

PETER. Well, I'm not sure you know that . . .

ANGELA. Sorry?

PETER. I think we're – me and Rachel are doing well – I mean, making progress –

ANGELA. Good, I hope I'm part of it too –

PETER. Yeah, but I'm pretty sure we're on the right track – I mean, me and Rachel have been talking quite seriously – I really feel we're getting somewhere – I mean, don't get any hopes up – but, you know, it's a start.

ANGELA. Good. That's – What have you been talking about?

PETER. There is something – I mean, you do come up quite a lot, and I think that's part of the problem you two are having –

ANGELA. You think I'm seeing too much of my daughter?

PETER. No. That doesn't matter that much. I suppose I'm just feeling very confident about it really – you know, I feel great about it really . . . I think I'm really helping – I'm, um, yeah.

ANGELA. Well. That's great.

RACHEL. I'm not asleep.

Beat.

ANGELA. Did we wake you, love?

RACHEL. No.

Pause.

ANGELA. Do you want me to go?

RACHEL. Put on the light.

PETER *puts the bedside lamp on.*

PETER. Hi.

Pause. Her face adjusts to the light.

RACHEL. Do you do this every night?

ANGELA. No.

RACHEL. This isn't a hospital. You shouldn't do that.

ANGELA. OK.

RACHEL. I mean it . . .

ANGELA. OK.

Pause. RACHEL *touches her scar, as if to reaffirm it's still there.*

RACHEL (*soft*). What were you saying . . . about Dad?

ANGELA. Oh. That. Well, I don't know if you remember him, carrying you up to bed.

RACHEL. I remember the game we used to do – 'Sack of Potatoes'.

ANGELA. Yes. That's right. He would get you in your
sleeping bag –

RACHEL. No, he'd put me in there and then he'd put me on
his back, in the bag, and go running around the room,
bouncing me off anything and then he'd put real salt in the
bag and shake it, and then he'd do this thing where he'd
pretend he didn't even like potatoes, so he'd tickle me.

PETER. Yeah?

RACHEL. He used to do an accent . . .

ANGELA. I did it too . . .

RACHEL. OK. Do it now.

ANGELA. I can't remember how it goes.

RACHEL. I think Peter thinks it was better that Dad died.
Because his didn't, his just fucked off.

PETER. No.

Pause.

ANGELA. Are you OK?

RACHEL. I don't even like HIM when you're here . . .
I remember you, before, and you were so not like any of
this . . . You were just much better before you became such
a wanker.

ANGELA. Rachel . . .

RACHEL. Don't pretend you're not pleased, Mum, you've got
no reason to be jealous now. He's just as crap as you are.

ANGELA. Rachel, don't be silly. I don't understand what
you're saying.

RACHEL. I knew you were the worst one before, Mum, and
now I'm not so sure. Listen to him.

PETER. I wasn't saying anything . . .

RACHEL. I'VE BEEN LISTENING TO YOU! I listened to
you. You were telling her all you'd done for me, like it was
some kind of an achievement.

ANGELA. It is, if you're getting better –

RACHEL. BUT I'M NOT! Am I? Where are my fucking legs
if I am getting better?

ANGELA. Rachel, it'll take time. Be fair.

RACHEL. NEITHER OF YOU ARE DOING ANYTHING!

ANGELA. I'd like to –

RACHEL. BUT YOU'RE FUCKING TALKING! I should go
to sleep now . . .

Pause.

ANGELA. Perhaps that is for the best.

PETER. Yeah.

RACHEL (*dangerous*). What?

Pause.

ANGELA. Do you want that light still on?

RACHEL. I can turn it off . . .

ANGELA. Sure?

RACHEL (*she demonstrates*). My hand can reach, thanks . . .

ANGELA. I don't even know what we've done . . .

Pause. ANGELA *exits,* PETER *follows her.*

PETER (*to* RACHEL). Bye.

ANGELA (*to* RACHEL). I love you.

RACHEL *looks to where her mum just left, and then turns
off the light.*

Pause. She shifts and looks in the opposite direction.

*She reaches a hand back and turns the light on again. She
keeps staring away from the door.*

Blackout.

ACT THREE

3.1

11th February.

PETER *puts his arms around her and pulls her up the bed. This is something they've done thousands of times now. She gets there and takes a breath and so does he.*

RACHEL. I wanted to be a nurse once.

PETER. Did you?

RACHEL. It was when I decided all jobs were selfish, because my mum was switching. I wanted to be a nurse or a police officer because they'd be the jobs I didn't want to do ever.

PETER. Really?

Pause.

(*He appraises what he is going to do.*) If we, um, twist you round, so that you'll be leaning against the – bedhead and then we put your feet on the ground. It's OK . . .

RACHEL. If it hurts, I want you to keep going anyway.

PETER. OK.

Pause. A moment's indecision, and then he gets to work. He twists her around, he puts her feet so they can touch the ground. This leaves her with her body cuddling up against the headboard of the bed. Her feet are floppy and useless, her back is twisted.

I wanted to be a politician.

RACHEL. What?

PETER. Yeah, I know. But my mum kept this badge I had made. I found it, recently, I mean, really recently – I was going to bring it in for you to look at.

RACHEL. But you changed your mind –

PETER. Yeah, I decided against it, I don't know why – I don't know, it's just a badge –

RACHEL. Who were you standing for? On the badge?

PETER (*throat laugh*). The Peter Party.

RACHEL. Really?

PETER. That's what the badge said –

RACHEL (*giggle*). What were your policies?

PETER. I don't think I had those. I think it was just vote for me, I'll make all the decisions when I have to, I think I mainly liked how the politicians dressed . . . The suits, you know . . .

RACHEL (*giggle*). Brilliant.

Pause. He sizes her up.

(*Looking at his anxiety.*) I think you should just keep going.

PETER. OK.

PETER *faces her like a weightlifter, full-on and strong, he pulls her hard up by her armpits, her feet are like puppets' feet, they don't find ground.*

(*Full of strain.*) Uh –

He lets her back down again, he has to try hard to not let his momentum cause him to fall into her. She tries to remain sitting, she doesn't want to go back to lying down. But this means as soon as he gets her down, she starts slipping off the bed, she can't get hold of enough of her headboard. She can't use her feet to arrest her ascent, and her back is exhausted, she makes a small squeak from her mouth as she slips.

PETER *catches her, or half-catches her, and part of her stays on the bed, and slowly, inch by inch, she regains balance and she's sitting again. Or grasping onto the headboard anyway.*

Pause. They both try and regain sense.

Pause. PETER *takes a tug on his inhaler.*

RACHEL. OK. Again?

PETER. Um –

RACHEL. If you're – we should –

PETER. Really?

RACHEL. Yeah.

PETER. OK.

He heaves her up by her armpits and takes the full weight of her on his body. His body isn't vertical, it's half-vertical, with his arse sticking out almost as a ballast. He grabs her around the waist, they're stuck in a horrible position. She is standing against him, she is totally leaning on him, but she's upright. This is an enormous strain for both of them. Her legs don't work to any degree.

(*Everything about him is strained.*) OK?

RACHEL. Yeah.

PETER. Sure?

RACHEL (*she's trying not to cry*). Yeah.

PETER. You think . . . can you try . . . standing . . .

RACHEL. No.

PETER. OK, time to get down . . .

He starts to waddle her back to the bed. He's using all his strength to lift her. But he can't move her far enough or fast enough. In a series of disjointed manoeuvres he puts her down on the floor. She makes another squeaking noise as he does. They haven't made it back to the bed. She lies on the floor, he hovers somewhere close.

(*He's desperately out of breath.*) Sorry.

RACHEL (*she's exhausted too*). OK.

He takes a squirt on his inhaler.

No rush, we can stay like this, I like it here . . .

PETER *coughs, he's exhausted. Pause.*

Can I lie in your lap? To get my head up . . .

PETER. Yeah?

RACHEL. OK?

He changes to a sitting position, and helps her put her head on his lap, he leans against the wall. Finally, they've found a comfortable pose, and they both relax as they realise that fact. They look nice together. PETER *coughs again and touches his chest where it hurts, but then he smiles.*

Can you reach my knee?.

PETER. Yeah.

RACHEL. Will you pinch it? Don't say when?

She covers her face with her hands. PETER *is slightly surprised. He thinks and then he moves to tweak her knee cautiously.*

(As he hovers his hand above, he doesn't make it.) Then?

PETER. No.

RACHEL. Try again . . .

PETER *moves quickly and tweaks her knee.*

I could feel your arm move . . .

PETER. OK.

Pause. She slumps into his lap.

RACHEL. I think we should go on a date.

PETER. What?

RACHEL. Just to the cinema, or ice skating, or dinner. Or a boat trip, just a canoe or . . . Somewhere nice, I think you should start saving up for it now. Sell all the boxes of chocolates people have sent me.

PETER. OK.

RACHEL. Yeah? Just somewhere nice, it doesn't have to be expensive, and I mean that – about the chocolates –

PETER. I think your mum will pay actually, she keeps trying to thrust money down my throat –

RACHEL (*keeping positive*). OK.

PETER. Yeah.

RACHEL. When we got together – did you think we'd last?

PETER. Yeah.

RACHEL. Good.

PETER. Yeah, I mean, how long?

RACHEL. How long did you think?

PETER. I was really chuffed when it happened though – I mean, you're really pretty. You still are.

She reaches her hand up past her scar, towards his throat.

RACHEL. Bring your – I want to touch your face . . .

He bullet-laughs.

I do. Can I?

PETER. Yeah

He moves his face down, she gently manipulates her hands over it.

RACHEL (*she moves her hands down over his shoulders, rubbing them*). Do you like this?

PETER. Yeah.

Pause. She smiles at him strangely.

(*Hmmph-laugh.*) What?

RACHEL. Bring your head down. Please. Peter.

PETER. I'm really sweaty . . .

He does, she holds onto his head with the back of her hand, again he's stuck in an odd position, their faces close together.

Pause. She takes his hand.

RACHEL. Smile.

PETER does.

Bring your face in, I wanted to see your smile really closer. Over my eyes. I want to smell your breath –

PETER (*trying to withdraw*). No.

RACHEL (*keeping him held in*). Come on . . .

PETER. No.

RACHEL (*she tries to pull his head down even closer*). Come on . . .

PETER (*he's really struggling quite hard*). Please. Ow!

RACHEL (*trying to pull her face up to meet his*). Come on . . .

PETER (*he forcibly dislocates her*). What's the MATTER with you . . .

Pause.

RACHEL. I want you to give me a bed bath –

PETER. What?

RACHEL. I'll tell you what to do.

Pause.

PETER. I think I should get you back on the bed.

RACHEL. Not yet.

Pause. A hoover starts on the stairs. As they talk, it slowly approaches the door, doing a stair at a time, RACHEL acts like she doesn't notice, but the hoover makes PETER even more nervous.

Will you give me a bed bath?

PETER. No. Of course not. Who normally does it? I'll get her.

RACHEL. Why?

Beat. The hoover is fast approaching.

PETER. The nurse or your mum should do it. Bath you.

RACHEL. I don't want them to.

PETER. When's the nurse next coming?

RACHEL. I don't want her to.

PETER. Then why do you want me to?

RACHEL. Because you're my boyfriend.

Pause. PETER *half-stutters out a laugh.*

You don't apologise much any more.

PETER. What?

RACHEL. You don't say sorry much any more.

PETER. Yeah?

RACHEL. Why does no one behave like I want them to . . .

PETER. I think I do, actually . . .

RACHEL. You're starting to smell like her too.

PETER. It smells in here actually . . .

RACHEL. Then give me my bed bath! Do you not want to see me?

Beat. The hoover is getting closer and closer.

You don't want to touch me . . . see my . . . see me.

PETER. No, I just think your mum would really like that.

RACHEL. I don't want my mum to perve on me.

Pause. The hoover switches off. RACHEL *smiles at that, and then frowns back at* PETER. *They don't say anything for a bit, and when they do, they speak quietly, as if someone's listening.*

PETER. I should get you back on the bed.

RACHEL. I like it here.

PETER *starts to manipulate her up.* RACHEL *resists as much as she can.*

No, Peter.

PETER (*looking towards the door*). SH!

RACHEL (*pushing his body hard away*). NO!

He gives up. He looks carefully at the door. Footsteps are heard going down the stairs.

PETER (*quiet and vicious*). You just want to stay on the floor?

RACHEL. Yes!

Pause.

It's normal to want to touch me . . .

PETER (*he's boiling hot*). I'm just like your mum / anyway . . .

RACHEL. That's what the problem is?

PETER. You said I was fucking useless . . .

RACHEL. So give me a bath!

PETER. Why did you say that to her like that?

RACHEL. You care what she thinks?

PETER. WE WERE GETTING BETTER!

RACHEL. WE FUCKING WEREN'T!

PETER. I WAS HELPING YOU!

RACHEL. FUCK OFF!

PETER. Look. LOOK, let's get you BACK on the BED . . .

RACHEL. I don't want that.

He starts to lift her.

I DON'T WANT THAT!

She pushes her hand up into his face. He keeps on trying to drag her up. She forces a hand into his eye, all the time wriggling her shoulders away from him.

PETER. Ow!

They size each other up, and then PETER *tries to lift her again, less apologetically this time, by her shoulders and elbows and whatever else he can manage. She grabs a*

*handful of his hair, pulls herself up to his level and she half-
headbutts him. They grapple.*

RACHEL (*quiet, concentrated on the effort*). Fucking . . .

*She manages to hit his head against the side of the bed.
Then she does it again, and it's harder this time. He pushes
her down onto the floor, hard, with the flat of his hand. She
bites his hand, and then tears at his hair and sticks her
elbow in his eye. He hits her down (he doesn't punch, it's
with the flat of his hand – he is determined to use the flat of
his hand wherever possible). She tries to tear at him again,
she scratches his eye.*

PETER. OW!

*She tries to pull at him again. He pushes hard, crack, against
the floor – and holds her there. Pinning her with his weight.*

STOP IT!

*She stops, like a toddler might stop. She doesn't seem to
understand what's going on, she just knows she's been hurt.
He dislocates himself away from her, pulls himself up to
sitting position. She's still lying on the floor. He fiddles in
his pocket and takes another tug on his inhaler. He coughs
repeatedly, and phlegm comes into his mouth, which he then
swallows. She doesn't say anything. It's ages before he
speaks.*

I . . . just . . . think it's not good . . . on the floor.

Pause.

RACHEL. I've worked out – I'd cover everything he could
breathe with – his mouth and – you can do ears too, breathe
through ears too. So I'd – just leave his nose. And then I'd
stand there and I'd just watch him, tied up with tape over
his mouth and his ears and anything he can breathe by.
I don't know whether you can breathe through the eyes –
I was quite surprised about the ear thing. And I'd have
a hammer with me, I'd just sit there mostly, but I'd have a
hammer. And every now and again I'd just tap him, his
nose, with the hammer, not to break it, just to remind him
that I had it, and he'd know that he could only breathe out

of his nose, because his mouth and ears are covered, so I'd just keep reminding him of it. And I'd tap it harder and harder but still tapping. Then I'd hit it harder, just so it'd sting or something, just so he really knew. It'd probably be really difficult for him to breathe then, but it'd come back to normal and we'd both wait for that, him and me. Just until it's completely right again. Then I'd break it. He'd probably still be able to breathe then but it'd hurt all the time. Then I'd hit it again until it was flat, his nose, and maybe that'd make him unconscious, the pain, or maybe he'd suffocate. But sometimes I think he's not too bad. I mean, just mixed up a bit, like you. Will you – bring your head down?

Pause.

I think I smell. I can smell myself, Peter. I can smell me, OK? My . . . I want you to wash me, I want you to see me.

PETER. Anyone can get you clean, if you smell . . . you don't smell . . .

Pause. PETER *scratches his hand and touches his eye gingerly. He starts to cry.*

(*Sniff.*) Why . . . Why did you follow him?

Beat.

No . . . I'm not accusing, I know there's a reason. If we're being honest.

Pause. PETER *stops crying.*

RACHEL. Will you touch my scar?

PETER (*the phlegm's back in his throat*). What?

RACHEL. To see if it hurts, it doesn't if I touch it, but I can never tell if that means anything . . .

PETER *bravely reaches out and touches it. She closes her eyes while he does.*

I was raped.

PETER. I know that. Look, I, uh, I think we share this . . . don't we?

RACHEL. Share what?

PETER. I just think if I don't understand something, I should ask.

RACHEL. Will you go away, Peter?

Beat.

I want you to go.

PETER. Fuck it. Sure.

RACHEL. Yeah?

PETER. You want me to go?

RACHEL. I don't want you to be so fucking gay about it as well.

Pause.

He quivers a moment, and then he leaves.

She listens to him go down the stairs. She tries to count his descent, under her breath.

She finishes counting, she reaches 21, she scratches the top of her arm.

She does nothing.

She hardly moves a muscle, she does nothing, she just lies there.

She counts to 21 again.

She gently fiddles with her eye, before reassuming neutral.

She smoothes down her arm.

She thinks. She looks at the side of the bed, and thinks about crawling up it.

She changes her mind, and puts her hand numbly inside her knickers.

She brings it out, checking to see if there's blood on it. There doesn't seem to be.

She smells her hand. She crumples her face as if ready to cry, but she doesn't.

She lies back, she tries to lie back as far as she can. But there isn't far to go.

She smells her hand again. This time there's more efficiency to how she does it.

She looks at her hand and traces the lines on her palm.

She scratches her hair.

She lies and waits.

She just lies there. Perfectly neutral.

An unmoving heavy mass. On the floor. Blackout.

3.2

14th February.

RACHEL *is back in bed and is being helped onto the bedpan by* ANGELA. RACHEL *pushes her knickers down to her mid-thighs, she's getting quite accomplished at this. Again it takes ages for* RACHEL *to start. There is a wheelchair leaning against the wall of the room.*

RACHEL. Ow –

ANGELA *lifts* RACHEL *up some more, to make sure she's firmly over the bedpan.*

ANGELA. When we get the wheelchair working, we'll be able to get you into the toilet.

RACHEL *says nothing.*

I'm your mother. It affects me too . . . I'm going to keep coming back until you're used to me . . .

RACHEL. Do you want me to kill myself?

ANGELA (*wiping something away with her shoulder, as she tightens her grip on* RACHEL*'s bum*). I keep thinking I've let you down . . .

RACHEL. I just don't like you here.

ANGELA. Why? Why can't we talk about this? I want to . . .

RACHEL. Because I DON'T WANT TO.

ANGELA. OK.

Pause.

They keep telling me – I phone Arsched – and he says, ask yourself the question 'What can I give this person?' And, uh . . . that I have to tell you that whatever response you have as a – survivor – is normal and I have to respect that . . . So I have to just have to be your – I just have to obey you until you change . . .

RACHEL. OK.

ANGELA. Rachel, when your dad died . . .

RACHEL. I don't want to talk about that.

ANGELA. OK.

Pause.

OK.

Pause. ANGELA *scratches her ear. Pause.*

Did I do something wrong?

RACHEL. Yes.

ANGELA. When?

RACHEL. The whole thing, OK?

ANGELA. They told me on the phone – they asked me 'Have you ever talked about sex with her?'

RACHEL. No –

ANGELA. It felt like they were accusing – but they said they weren't and I thought all that was done at school now – well, I know we needed to talk about it, but you were never an easy person to talk to – I mean – but if we had talked about it then it might have meant we could talk about this –

RACHEL. Wait –

Pause.

RACHEL *starts to pee. This time the dribble is not so painful. It sounds almost normal.*

She farts accidentally. They both keep very still.

They wait for more.

It doesn't come.

ANGELA. I want to talk to you about it, Rachel.

RACHEL (*muffled*). No.

ANGELA. Just tell me what happened.

RACHEL. NO!

ANGELA. Who would do that to a little girl?

RACHEL. I'm not a little girl.

ANGELA. I think –

RACHEL (*turning as far as she can towards her mum*). I DON'T CARE.

Pause. A final dribble, RACHEL makes a slight growling noise, this takes some effort.

ANGELA *waits for more,* RACHEL *concentrates on her bladder.*

There's nothing left.

You can go, Mum . . .

ANGELA. Have you finished?

RACHEL. Yes.

ANGELA. You just wanted a wee, did you . . .

Beat. RACHEL *says nothing.*

ANGELA *checks she's steady and then hands her the toilet paper. She attempts to break the paper off for her daughter, but is stopped from doing so.*

RACHEL *uses it aggressively. She dumps the paper in the pan, this causes an involuntary spasm in her back.*

ANGELA *doesn't notice* RACHEL*'s pain.*

RACHEL *refocuses on her mother. She pulls up her own knickers.*

RACHEL. I hate you doing this . . . At least Peter didn't like doing it . . .

ANGELA. Let's just make this easy . . .

RACHEL *is helped off the bedpan.* ANGELA *carries it out of the room. Having a quick glance at it as she does.*

RACHEL *waits in silence, she keeps entirely still. She tries not to blink.*

ANGELA *re-enters, she's now washed the bedpan. She puts it back under the bed and picks up* RACHEL*'s used dinner tray and carries it out.*

It was nice, that, wasn't it?

RACHEL. If Peter comes back, you're not to say anything, yeah? If he is –

ANGELA. About what?

RACHEL. About anything, Mum. I don't want you to speak to him at all. He's my friend.

ANGELA (*slumping slightly*). OK.

RACHEL *doesn't say anything, despite* ANGELA*'s pathetic eyes. So* ANGELA *exits.*

Nothing. A big crowd of it.

Nothing.

More nothing. RACHEL *tries not to move. She has a system worked out for her first few moments of peace. It's a tried and tested system and generally involves anaesthetising herself with great big silences. Blackout.*

3.3

20th February.

ALICE *is sitting there diligently.* RACHEL *has her back turned to her.*

ALICE. Have you been reading anything?

RACHEL. No.

ALICE. We've got this crap book we've got to read for English. What do you do then? Most of your time? Without a TV. I mean, when you're here.

RACHEL. You think I leave at night?

ALICE. What?

RACHEL. What?

　Pause.

　You think I leave at night?

ALICE. Are your feet getting better then?

RACHEL. What?

ALICE. I don't understand.

RACHEL. You said 'when I'm here'.

ALICE. What?

RACHEL. When am I not?

ALICE. No. I just . . . Have I said something wrong?

　RACHEL *turns over, this takes some effort, to face* ALICE.

　Um. The musical is going well. I've got promoted.

RACHEL. OK.

ALICE. I still haven't told James though, isn't that pathetic? Still, I've been thinking a lot about that, since we spoke, and we just aren't that kind of couple, you know. I mean, he's amazing in bed. I mean, actually, isn't it funny that

that's embarrassing? I mean, it wasn't great to start with but now it's nice – loving, you know. It's funny. I don't know. Have you seen Peter?

RACHEL (*laugh, funny voice*). I thought I left him with you.

ALICE. No. He's not in school. James went to see him, but he wasn't in. His mum was a bitch to James actually. Told him off for leaving his bike on the lawn.

Pause.

Is that a wheelchair?

RACHEL. Yes.

ALICE. Oh. Suzy's split up with –

RACHEL. – I don't know them.

ALICE. Um. I wasn't sure how long to leave it before coming back. I wasn't . . .

RACHEL. Yeah. What do you want to talk about?

ALICE. There's nothing . . . I can do or anything . . .

RACHEL. Do you know why my real friends aren't here? Because they asked, and I said no. They asked me whether I wanted them here, and I didn't . . .

ALICE. Do you want me to tell them to come over?

RACHEL. Did you not hear what I said?

ALICE. You sounded like you'd changed your mind.

RACHEL. You want to make an announcement in assembly, don't you? 'Rachel's ready to receive visitors she was nasty to before. She's OK now.'

ALICE. No. I just thought you might want someone round here . . .

RACHEL. Why? To entertain me . . .

ALICE. Well, it's not exactly entertaining you, is it? It's just chatting really . . .

RACHEL. Depends how clever you are . . .

ALICE (*completely crushed – with a big smile*). Have I done something wrong? I mean, I liked it . . . here . . .

RACHEL. We don't have anything to talk about . . .

ALICE. Yeah, but we can talk about loads of stuff, music, things like that . . .

RACHEL. I don't LIKE that stuff . . .

ALICE. James isn't going to come barging in again. I had such a go at him about that.

Beat.

When you said – about the virginity thing – I wasn't really – when I, it wasn't like he asked or anything. I mean, it wasn't bad or anything like that, but he just didn't really ask. And it is entirely different, I mean, James, I'm in love with him, so when he did it, it was fine. And I didn't say no or anything like that, because it was really surprising, and I had to go and get the twenty-four-hour thing. But it was so weird, you know? I wanted to say, that I wasn't sure when I was going to – I wanted to save it a little bit too. I don't think it's that odd really, wanting to stay a virgin, I mean, I'd have quite liked that. He said afterwards it was an accident, well, he said it like I made a mistake but then we kept doing it after that. Like that had been the first for real rather than an accident.

Pause.

RACHEL. Do you want me to say something?

ALICE. No.

RACHEL. Good.

Pause.

ALICE (*with honour*). You still want me to go?

RACHEL. Yes.

ALICE. Do I come back?

RACHEL. No.

ALICE. OK.

She picks up her things, she walks out of the room.

Um. I'm not upset. OK? Don't worry. I'll see you when you're better . . . OK? And maybe we can talk. OK?

ALICE *exits. We hear the clatter of her going down the stairs.* ALICE'*s heels sound more aggressive now.*

RACHEL *sits in silence, she scratches her eyelid.*

Blackout.

3.4

28th February.

ANGELA *has partially lifted up* RACHEL, *and* RACHEL *is also getting leverage by the use of her arms.* ANGELA *is pulling the sheet from under* RACHEL. *This is a complicated but highly efficient procedure.*

RACHEL. Ow –

ANGELA *lifts* RACHEL *up some more, but keeps pulling the sheet.*

That's OK.

ANGELA. OK.

ANGELA *starts to put a new sheet on the bed. She does so in silence. This is even more of an effort,* RACHEL'*s bum has to be lifted up while the sheet is shunted underneath her.*

RACHEL. Ow.

ANGELA *finishes and starts filling up a washing basket with* RACHEL'*s clothes from the floor.*

ANGELA. You're almost out of knickers.

RACHEL. Because most of those are clean . . .

ANGELA. What?

RACHEL. You're washing clean knickers.

ANGELA *sniffs a pair that she's just put in the basket, the knickers are dirty and smell. She adds them to the basket, while* RACHEL *giggles. Pause.* ANGELA *continues putting washing in the basket, as if she hadn't noticed. Then she stops and looks carefully at her daughter. Pause.* RACHEL *looks carefully back. She wipes her cheek roughly, she's not crying, but her cheeks are hot. She's melting slightly.*

I don't want to be like this . . .

Beat.

ANGELA (*trying not to rush over*). I know you don't, love . . .

RACHEL. I . . . um . . . I want to be nicer now . . .

ANGELA. Well, nice isn't so important, but let's get you in the chair, let's be positive . . .

RACHEL. Not the chair.

ANGELA. The chair will be so useful.

RACHEL. Mum, you're saying the wrong things, OK? I want to be nicer, OK?

Pause.

ANGELA. OK.

Pause. ANGELA *scratches her ear. Pause.*

Do you want to talk to me?

RACHEL. Not yet. But I will.

ANGELA. That's good. That's a relief.

RACHEL. Don't cry.

ANGELA. No, I won't. I do love you, you know that?

RACHEL. Yes, I know that.

Pause.

ANGELA. Do you want me to phone any of your friends?

RACHEL. Not yet.

ANGELA. OK. And we'll try the chair eventually, will we?

RACHEL. I want to do that slowly.

ANGELA. OK.

The doorbell rings.

Good.

RACHEL. Don't make a big deal out of it, OK?

ANGELA. No, I won't, I'm just pleased . . .

RACHEL. Good. I'm pleased too.

The doorbell rings again. ANGELA *flinches.*

ANGELA. Shall I get that?

RACHEL. Yes.

ANGELA. I am pleased, love, OK?

RACHEL. I'm pleased too.

ANGELA. OK.

ANGELA exits. Nothing.

More nothing.

RACHEL shifts her shoulder, and tries to make it touch the other side of the bed. We can hear someone walking slowly up the stairs.

They take ages. RACHEL *starts to try and pull herself up the bed. She gets her muscles in a tangle, she gets caught with her right arm acting as pivot at a funny angle.*

JAMES enters the room.

JAMES. Your mum let me up . . .

RACHEL. OK.

JAMES. Yeah. She seemed really pleased to see me actually. I mean . . .

RACHEL. Can you just – I need a hand – will you –

JAMES *leans over and supports her back.* RACHEL *re-adjusts her arm. She's comfortable.*

JAMES (*with one of his smiles*). Hi.

Blackout.

ACT FOUR

4.1

6th March.

She's asleep. PETER *stands about five metres from her bed. He makes as if to move, to sit down. But changes his mind and just remains standing proud.*

He doesn't say anything.

Pause.

PETER. Rach?

He sits down, and then stands up again, and moves backwards from the bed.

Pause. He notices the wheelchair and walks over and touches it. He then turns away from it as if spotted. He is prowling.

He takes off his jumper, he struggles with it slightly.

Rachel . . . Rach?

RACHEL (*growling with post-sleep*). Con . . .

PETER. Hi.

Pause. She registers him, she pulls back.

Hi. I, uh, I'm –

Pause. She tries to shift away from him. She's still slightly asleep.

Hi. Rachel?

Pause.

I just really wanted . . . to talk to you. Your mum's making dinner, so I thought . . . you'd need to be awake in a bit, if

you like . . . Do you still want that bed bath? I thought it'd
be good to wash – (*Half-laugh.*) before dinner.

*Pause. He scratches himself and waits. She turns and looks
at him.*

Hi.

RACHEL. OK.

Pause. RACHEL *tries to sit up, he moves as if to help her,
but she knows what she's doing now. She puts a pillow from
her head underneath her back. Then she pulls herself up
using hands on the bedboard, the pillow getting lower and
lower down her back as she does. Finally she's in semi-
sitting position.* PETER *watches this in awed silence.*

Pause. She looks at him carefully, he looks back.

PETER. Oh. I saw the maddest thing . . . I was walking, when
I was going . . . home . . . A man was sitting in his car,
listening to his radio. It wasn't that strange. But he looked
pretty intense. I thought he was probably listening to the
football or something, or he'd had an argument and gone
outside to sit in the car. I don't know, but it felt really
strange. And then I got scared he was gassing himself, and
that I didn't notice, so I went back to check, and he noticed
I was checking and smiled at me. It wasn't that mad, it felt
pretty strange. He was probably listening to the football.

Pause.

And I've given up the football team . . . county, I mean . . .
Baylis was really pissed off – 'the first school representative
for years' – but it was making me feel too important.

RACHEL (*quiet*). Where have you been?

PETER. I don't know. Listen. Can I do anything? I mean, it
doesn't have to be –

RACHEL. OK. (*Beat.*) You need to buy me some tampons.

PETER. OK.

RACHEL. I just don't want to ask Mum. She'll just fuss, she
got me some last week, but I'm . . .

PETER. I'll get them. Is there a particular sort? Or . . .

RACHEL. Whatever's cheapest. Heavy flow.

PETER. Heavy flow, OK.

RACHEL. Take the money out of my top drawer?

PETER. No. I can get it.

RACHEL. Peter –

PETER. No. I've got it. Is there any particular – brand – you prefer?

RACHEL. You want to buy me tampons as a present?

PETER. No.

RACHEL begins to giggle, PETER *joins in. She then stops, and looks careful again.*

I'm just pleased you want me back. To give them to you . . .

RACHEL. Arsched said to say like you weren't coming back – think like –

PETER. Well, he was wrong. I want to be back –

RACHEL. Why?

PETER. Because I want to be . . . I think that's a pretty good reason . . .

Pause. RACHEL *shifts her bum slightly, using her hands,* PETER *notices.*

Is it urgent? Do you want me to get them now?

RACHEL. Yeah. I'm bleeding all over the bed.

Pause. He moves his foot and then regrets it.

PETER. Your mum seemed pleased to see me. Though you've been talking, the two of you, yeah?

RACHEL. Did you know James came round?

PETER. Yeah?

RACHEL. He said you hadn't been in school . . . for a while.

PETER. No.

RACHEL. He asked whether he could do anything. I said, 'How's Alice?' and he got really defensive about that because I'd been a bitch to her when she came round – I said I thought you fancied her and he laughed.

PETER. No.

RACHEL. He said that he'd told you that we hadn't been together long enough for all this – effort –

Pause.

He said he'd said to you he didn't think I was worth it – all this trouble, all this effort and stuff you're doing. He said he didn't want you doing it all just because you felt you had to or because you felt sorry for me and that he had told you that, and that it was unfair of me to expect so much of you. Because it wasn't your fault I'm like this. You weren't doing enough other stuff, other than me, I was basically sort of eating you up. He said he wasn't going behind my back, he wasn't that kind of guy, anything he said to you about me, he wanted to say to my face as well. So he did – he came round to see me just so he wasn't talking behind my back. Which is quite an effort, just so you aren't talking behind someone's back. You're his best friend so he felt he should stick up for you, or help you, or say things to me about you – um . . . I think he was quite worried about you – being missing. So, anyway, that was all funny – considering what I know about him and Alice. Do you think there's something wrong with him and Alice? Because I do. Anyway, I thought it was quite brave of him. Though I can't stand up so . . .

PETER (*close*). He shouldn't have said that.

RACHEL. Was that what you were thinking? Were you –

PETER. No. No. I mean, we're not that – we're not that – close – any more –

RACHEL (*soft, quick*). Me and you?

PETER. No. No. James.

RACHEL. Is Alice the reason you argued?

PETER. No. You. Listen, what he said –

RACHEL. She likes you, I think – James is quite rough. Some of the things she said.

PETER. Yeah? But I'm here with you.

RACHEL. But I think most of the stuff is stuff she does. She basically tells him to treat her like shit. She's that kind of girl . . .

PETER. No. She's not.

RACHEL. Do you fancy her?

PETER. No . . . I fancy you.

Beat.

RACHEL (*quiet*). Do you want to give me that bed bath?

PETER. OK.

Beat. He lets go of her leg. Neither of them look at each other.

RACHEL (*nervous, but with a brilliant face on it*). You need to go and get a – there's a basin in the bathroom with a sponge in it and some special soap, fill that up, fill it in the bath, or using the shower otherwise it'll take ages –

PETER. OK.

He hesitates and then exits, RACHEL *waits.*

She doesn't try and do anything, she just waits, steely-eyed.

Pause. She scratches her nose, touches her scar, smells her hand.

Pause.

Finally, PETER *re-enters, clutching the basin, careful not to spill it.*

RACHEL. Put it on the floor.

PETER. OK.

RACHEL. Have you put the soap in the water?

PETER. I wasn't sure to – before I poured it – you said it was special soap so . . .

RACHEL. Put some in now, it's fine.

PETER. I could do it again.

RACHEL. No. Don't.

Beat. PETER *adds soap to the water, and then swirls it round.*

Get the sponge wet.

PETER *does.*

Really squeeze it out, as much as you can.

PETER. OK.

RACHEL. Now just sponge me down . . .

PETER. You don't just want to do it yourself . . .

Beat. She undoes her straps, ready for the top to be taken off. He watches.

RACHEL. I could do my front if you want . . .

PETER. OK.

RACHEL (*forced giggle*). But that's the best bit . . .

PETER. No. You can do it.

RACHEL. I want you to do it.

PETER. Can I do your back first?

RACHEL. Yeah. Help me turn.

He helps her. Then he starts to wipe her back carefully with the cloth. He does so very methodically, lifting up her arms and her hair to get to the places where he thinks she needs cleaning.

Alice likes you, I think, James is quite . . . rough. Some of the things she said.

PETER. Yeah?

RACHEL. But I think most of it is stuff she does. She basically tells him to treat her like shit, she's that kind of girl . . .

PETER. I think that's . . . done.

RACHEL. Turn me over then.

With his help, she turns over onto her front. She makes to cover her breasts, but then changes her mind and makes them as exposed as possible.

PETER. You don't need your face . . .

RACHEL. No.

He carefully wipes down her body, they hardly breathe. He eventually finishes, he's being so careful, it's beautiful. He finishes and they sit in silence.

PETER. We should get you walking after this . . .

RACHEL. I've got a wheelchair now.

PETER. Yeah. I saw, I thought that was . . . great.

Beat. PETER *gingerly moves forward and puts* RACHEL's *straps back on, he hides her breasts for her. She lets him.*

RACHEL. What did you really do? When you weren't in school.

PETER. Oh. Um. Walked about. There was a pub where I played the slots a bit. I lost a bit. But . . . I just walked about mostly, went into shops. But, uh . . .

RACHEL. Why did you put my straps back on?

PETER. I don't know.

RACHEL. OK. Now you need to do the bottom half.

PETER. I know.

Pause. They just look at each other.

RACHEL. There's no. Blood.

PETER. Yeah, OK . . .

RACHEL. Help me turn over again . . .

PETER. OK.

He tries to help her turn over, but doesn't want to put much effort into it.

RACHEL. Peter –

He tries again, this time, she turns easily. He lifts up her gown, she pulls her knickers down to her mid-thighs and he, thinking it's a hint, pulls them all the way off and places them beside her on the bed. She says nothing and he starts slowly to clean her. Very, very gently. Then, after he finishes that side, he wordlessly half-lifts her and pulls her back onto her front and then cleans her some more, going all the way down to her feet, he spends a lot of time on her feet. Then he finishes.

PETER. Done.

RACHEL. OK, just, uh, go to the bathroom and pour it all away. Just leave it how you found it.

PETER. Who did you last time?

RACHEL. The nurse did me a couple of times, then my mum . . .

PETER. OK.

He picks up the basin and exits. RACHEL pulls herself down in the bed, so she's back in lying position. She checks her body, all over, with her hand. PETER re-enters.

RACHEL. Sit on the bed, would you?

PETER. I don't . . .

RACHEL. Lie down, with me, please . . .

PETER hesitates, then gets on the bed.

I want to be facing you . . .

PETER. OK.

PETER turns her, helps her turn, and then lies down beside her, so that the two of them are facing each other, she strokes his face.

RACHEL. Can I tell you something –

PETER. Yeah.

RACHEL. I followed him because I was scared –

PETER. No. I didn't mean that . . . question. It wasn't a question.

RACHEL. But I don't want those questions with you –

PETER. I know.

RACHEL. When they first did the photofit – he looked like my dad.

PETER. Oh.

RACHEL. I couldn't get it right. (*Laugh.*) The police wanted to talk to him until they found out . . . he was dead.

PETER. OK.

RACHEL. When they showed me the photofit – they said – does that remind you of anyone and I said, 'Yes,' because I realised and they said, 'Who?' And I said, 'That reminds me of my dad.' So they just said, 'Is your dad still at home with you? Billy, can you call the social in?' And I said, 'My dad's dead,' and I saw Billy – the one they call Billy, I didn't really know him – almost laugh. Because it was quite funny. So I smiled at him, and he just tried to stop laughing, I mean, he didn't let it out. They were really disappointed. And I didn't want you there, to see that, or . . . anything. I was rubbish at it.

Beat.

Take off your top.

PETER. Now?

RACHEL. I like your chest.

He takes off his top, he struggles a bit. It's difficult taking off your top when you're lying down.

I followed him because I thought if I did anything else then he'd be worse and I didn't put up much of a fight the rest of the time either. And I – when I talked about that stuff, with Arsched, the police, the doctors – I didn't want you there because I was ashamed and I was bad at it. Peter, I couldn't even tell them what he looked like – so / I made him look like my dad . . .

PETER. I knew that. I wasn't –

RACHEL. Do you mind if I undo my straps? I want to feel me and you . . .

PETER. OK.

She undoes her straps halfway.

RACHEL. I don't want to have sex.

PETER. No.

RACHEL. It's OK. I'm still not . . . ready.

PETER. Yeah.

RACHEL. OK.

Pause, she undoes the remainder of her straps. Then they lie there, in an odd but perfectly formed shape. They try not to breathe.

(*Soft.*) I don't think I'd be able to . . . feel it . . . anyway . . . sometimes I can feel it though, when I pee . . . so . . .

PETER. Yeah?

RACHEL. But I don't think I'd feel it and that would be . . .

PETER. Yeah.

RACHEL. When it's our first time, I want it to be about us . . . Not . . . I don't want things left to chance.

PETER. No. I'm not – ready – either . . .

Pause. PETER *clears his throat.*

RACHEL. I'm sorry you won't be . . . first.

PETER. No. That's OK.

RACHEL. This feels amazing.

PETER. Yeah.

RACHEL. I love you.

Beat.

Will you take your trousers off . . .

PETER. I'm . . .

RACHEL. That's OK, I'm expecting it.

PETER *does. This takes him a minute, he's not sure how to do it.*

Will you help me take everything off . . .

PETER. OK.

They pull her nightie over her head, there's a brief moment of tangle, but then it's all OK.

RACHEL. This feels amazing, doesn't it?

PETER. I love you too.

RACHEL. OK.

Beat.

PETER. Are you OK?

RACHEL. No. This is good for me. I think. This is –

PETER. Are you, uh . . .

RACHEL. I think I can feel you, in my legs, I think I can feel your legs.

PETER. Can you?

RACHEL. Do you want to take your boxer shorts off?

PETER. No.

RACHEL. OK. Kiss me.

He does. She ventures a hand down his body.

PETER. No. Don't.

RACHEL. It's just a hand.

PETER. No. Don't.

They lie together forever. The Archers theme music starts playing from downstairs, RACHEL *giggles through her snot.*

Pause.

(*Soft.*) Are you – crying?

RACHEL. This is better. We'll stay like this – OK?

PETER. Yeah.

RACHEL. It'll be worth it soon – I'll let you – we can make love –

PETER. No. That's not important –

RACHEL. Well, now you know anyway –

PETER. No –

RACHEL. Cuddle me – now you know –

PETER. OK.

RACHEL. Tighter –

PETER. OK . . .

RACHEL. I love you.

PETER. I love you too.

Long pause. She tries to feel closer to him.

RACHEL. I want to turn over, I want you around me, is that OK? I want you tucked up into me. I don't mind. If I can feel anything . . . I don't mind that . . .

Beat.

PETER. OK.

He effects some of this, their bodies spoon. He tries to hold his groin as far away from her as possible. That's an almost impossible task. She tries to nestle in. Then tries again. Then tries a third time. She looks confused, and then upset.

RACHEL. This feels nice.

PETER. Yeah.

She nestles in a fourth time. Moving her back down to him.

RACHEL. You're not . . .

PETER. No. Not yet.

RACHEL. It's gone down?

Pause. PETER *tries again to move away from her, but there's no room for that.* RACHEL's *permi-smile fades.*

I was just expecting it . . .

PETER. Yeah?

RACHEL (*soft*). It wasn't something . . . I did?

PETER. No.

Pause. She picks up his forearm and studies it, he tries to lean over her to see what she's doing, but he can't. Again, it's difficult him being on the bed.

RACHEL (*small*). You do still fancy me?

PETER. Yeah.

She traces a few of the lines on his hand.

RACHEL. I know I don't look amazing . . . but . . . It doesn't matter. We can be friends.

PETER. No, we're – you're my girlfriend.

RACHEL (*perfectly soft*). Has anyone tried anything?

PETER. What?

RACHEL. Any of the other girls? Libby? Nicky? Ruth?

PETER. No.

RACHEL (*a delicious forced giggle*). They will. You're quite fanciable really. I should do an erection test. Say their name, describe what they look like, and I know them naked, see if you get one . . . Libby – let's see – at a guess, 32C – big, long nipples, she walks around naked in the girl's dressing rooms, though her arse is bigger than you'd expect.

She tried to shave herself once, and cut it . . . Alice, short stubby nipples, no room, Libby's spread out, hers don't . . . this stomach which tips slightly over her knickers, not fat, muscle . . . this perfect arse . . . (*They both stiffen.*) OK. That's OK.

PETER. I'm getting off the bed.

RACHEL. No! DON'T! No!

He half-falls and half-dismounts the bed.

Pause. He's trying to hold in his erection.

PETER. Sorry.

Pause. She isn't sure what to do.

RACHEL. Do you want a blow job? I think I could do one of those. Do you? You'll have to come closer.

Pause.

I don't mind, Peter. Honestly.

PETER. No.

Pause. He starts to shuffle back away from her, and then stops. They stand there for ages.

Listen – (*Soft.*) Do you really think I can help?

RACHEL. Help what?

PETER. You.

RACHEL. You're supposed to want to see me.

PETER. Yeah?

RACHEL. I think I understand why you're going better than you do.

PETER. No, I'm not . . . leaving . . .

Pause. RACHEL *touches her scar.*

RACHEL. You should stop being friends with James –

PETER. I know.

RACHEL. But don't . . . Alice – don't rescue her – because she doesn't need it – that's just the way she is – girly, she's not really worth much . . . She enjoys being a victim too much. Plastic.

PETER. That wasn't Alice, the erection, it wasn't you talking about Alice. It was you, I mean, lying with you, and you kept sticking your bum harder into me when you were telling me about how . . . I mean, you could have been talking about anyone naked, it was really nice . . . and just so, with your bum sticking into me. I think you're really pretty, and it was you that gave me the . . . I'm not put off, and no one . . . That's what my mum thought, but that's not what . . .

RACHEL. OK. Thanks.

PETER. No. No. Don't say thanks.

Pause. RACHEL*'s shoulders slump, gradually and completely. Until there's almost nothing left.*

RACHEL (*slow and soft*). I . . . I never really liked it when you were here – we always got it wrong, didn't we? I liked you visiting for the bits in between – the bits when you weren't here – when I could dream or plan your next visit – when I could – you're really good to dream about, Peter, you're that kind of person. So it didn't matter when your visits were shit because they were only two or three hours long – or one hour sometimes – and there were twenty or thirty or forty hours in between your visits and I used to just think about you – about how we'd get it right next time. You filled up my brain – and that was – great – when I was just waiting – to get better. Even when you weren't here for thirty days – you filled up my . . . So – thank you – I'm really grateful for that. I liked thinking about you – sometimes I thought the wrong thing but . . . you were the good bit. Most of the time, you were something good to think about. So don't be hard on yourself, OK? You did really well.

Beat. He moves his body as if to sit on the bed. But he doesn't move his feet.

But the thing is . . . I think maybe, if I'm going to get better –
I'm going to have to do it without all this . . . effort. I
just want to make everything normal. I'm not sure you can
be . . . make me normal – I'm not sure the effort you make
me . . . is the right kind. I am really grateful though . . .

Pause.

Did you ever even want to be here?

PETER (*careful, in case he gets the words wrong*). I want to be
here now.

Beat. She turns some of her body away from him.

RACHEL (*tired*). OK.

The lights slowly fade, PETER *just stands there, in his
boxers, unsure whether to put his clothes on again or not.*

Blackout.

Music: 'If You Could See Her' from Cabaret.

End.